The **Essential** Buyer's Guide

JAGUAR
X-TYPE
Model years 2001 to 2009

T0168166

Your marque expert:
Nigel Thorley

VELOCE PUBLISHING
THE PUBLISHER OF FINE AUTOMOTIVE BOOKS

www.veloce.co.uk

First published in November 2012 by Veloce Publishing Limited, Veloce House, Parkway Farm Business Park, Middle Farm Way, Poundbury, Dorchester, Dorset, DT1 3AR, England.
Fax 01305 250479/e-mail info@veloce.co.uk/web www.veloce.co.uk or www.velocebooks.com.

ISBN: 978-1-845844-62-2 UPC: 6-36847-04462-6

Introduction
– the purpose of this book

The cars covered in this publication, the Jaguar X-Type models, were produced for a relatively short period from 2001, initially as petrol-engined saloons only, with diesel and estate versions becoming available later. The X-Type represented a major change for Jaguar, producing a much smaller car to supposedly satisfy a new market for the brand.

The launch of the X-Type came in 2001 after much speculation by the motoring world about what the car would look like. On the one hand, the X-Type heralded an entirely new model, adding a fourth car to the range (alongside the flagship XJ, medium-sized S-Type and Sports XK models), but at the same time, because of its conservative styling, it suited many existing Jaguar customers who wanted to downsize.

However, from Jaguar's point of view the X-Type was aimed squarely at the market dominated by the BMW 3 Series, although it was also hoping to win over customers from the likes of Mercedes, Audi, and many other mainstream brands like VW, Peugeot, Honda, and even Ford.

Because of Ford's ownership of the Jaguar company at the time, and to save money on development and components, many attributes of the X-Type came directly from the parent company and its existing models, like the Ford Mondeo. Styling, however, was Jaguar's domain, taking cues from the successful XJ models.

The X-Type was launched with the existing 3.0-litre V6 unit, adapted from the larger S-Type saloon, along with a smaller 2.5-litre version of the same engine. Both models featured all-wheel drive, the first Jaguars to do so. Later, an even smaller 2.0-litre petrol V6 engine was available, supposedly to cater for the fleet market, and then diesel models were introduced, initially of 2.0-litre capacity, with a 2.2-litre unit available later.

An estate version became available mid-way through production – the first ever production estate car produced by Jaguar – and it proved an incredible success.

Although the X-Type has been out of production since 2009 (many cars were registered as late as 2010) and, at the time of writing, has not been replaced by an equivalent model, the car has retained a very strong following with existing owners and those looking to buy a smaller, economical Jaguar saloon/estate car. Existing owners look to upgrade to later models, while first-time Jaguar buyers look to the X-Type as a low-cost entry level car into the brand. Even Jaguar enthusiasts now consider the X-Type a worthy model to carry the name, with many using an X-Type as everyday transport while keeping their more cherished cars for occasional use.

At the time of writing, many cars are still looked after by the Jaguar franchised dealerships, but a significant number of independent Jaguar specialists have been set up to maintain these cars. There are also many aftermarket modifications and accessories available for the model, plus strong support for the car via the internet and Jaguar clubs worldwide.

There has never been a better time to consider buying one of these cars, with plenty of choice at some very reasonable prices. This publication is your first step to ownership: a comprehensive guide to what to look for and how to go about buying one.

Contents

The Essential Buyer's Guide™ currency

At the time of publication a BG unit of currency "●" equals approximately £1.00/US$1.62/Euro 1.26. Please adjust to suit current exchange rates using Sterling as the base currency.

Tall and short drivers

The Jaguar X-Type models were built on an entirely new floorpan and bodyshell, very different to any other Jaguar models, but allied to contemporary Ford Mondeo architecture. As such the design was well thought out, so front seat passengers should have no problem in finding sufficient space, with more than adequate adjustment in the seats. Even with cars fitted with sunroofs there have never been any reports of drivers finding difficulty in getting comfortable, or with headroom.

Rear seat passengers are reasonably well accommodated for but one has to remember that this is a small car by Jaguar standards, so expect some constraints although it is no less spacious than other contemporary cars of this size.

Weight of controls

The car is not only relatively light but feels light and easy to handle. All cars have power-assisted steering and brakes, and the majority of the controls fall easily to hand.

Will it fit in the garage?

Only one wheelbase applied to all models with a slight difference in length from saloon to estate.
    Length: 183in (4868mm) saloon/186in (4724mm) estate
    Width: 68in (1727mm)
    Height: 53in (1346mm) saloon model

Interior space

Space in the X-Type is good, if not overly abundant. Seats are well proportioned and the interior is generally light and airy.

The X-Type interior is well designed, providing ample space and comfort for all drivers.

Luggage capacity

Boot space is well designed with a low loading area, a wide opening, and a boot lid that extends quite high for ease of access. The spare wheel does not intrude as it is stowed below the boot floor. Most saloons have fold down rear seating allowing for larger items to be easily accommodated in the boot area.

The estate car is quite cavernous with a wide top hinged tailgate that has a separate top glass section, which may be opened separately. The rear seats fold down for extended storage space, the boot floor is totally flat and there is even extra storage space under the estate car floor.

Storage capacity inside the car is limited to shallow door pockets, a passenger side glove box plus a small centre console armrest compartment for front seat passengers (plus one for rear seat passengers).

Rear accommodation is adequate.

Luggage accommodation in the boot/trunk is good, with little restriction.

Running costs

All the petrol engines are quite economical by the standards of this size of car. Average fuel consumption figures of above 30mpg can easily be achieved and it is not unusual to obtain over 40mpg on a long run under controlled conditions. The diesel engines are even more economical and it has been known for some owners to extract over 50mpg, particularly with the 6-speed manual transmission 2.2-litre model.

Normal servicing costs are not high with 10,000 mile intervals, but extra maintenance on items like gearbox oil/filter changes can raise the bills considerably. Diagnosing problems can be an issue for the DIY mechanic without specialist equipment.

Usability

A very practical car in all conditions. Is it to be a car for occasional or everyday use, and what mileage will be covered? Don't buy a diesel if it is to be subjected to very low mileages over short distances – It won't pay, and could present problems!

Parts availability

There are very few known parts availability problems for these models at the time of going to print. Accident damaged and cheaper cars beyond repair do find their way to specialist dismantlers, where stocks of used parts can already be found, which are usually guaranteed.

Parts cost

Being a modern car, many items are still only available directly from Jaguar and are not cheap. There is always the tendency for some garages to replace, rather than attempt to repair items, which can prove more costly.

Overall, Jaguar parts prices are at least as cheap as many other contemporary models from other manufacturers. However, there are major costs with drive trains, etc. which can prove prohibitive if the car is not worth a lot of money to start with!

Insurance

Insurance costs can be cheaper than you would think. Being a member of a Jaguar club can provide access to specialist schemes with discounts for limited use, multiple vehicles, etc.

Investment potential

Not at present, and it has to be remembered that even as cars become classics, the saloons and estates never appreciate to the same degree as sporting models. However, these cars are already well respected and offer superb value for money, particularly for enthusiasts of the brand, who haven't owned a Jaguar before. Late models, particularly estates, are the most sought after.

Alternatives

Rivals have tended to be the Mercedes C Class, Audi A4, VW Passat and even top end models from the likes of Mazda, Toyota, etc, plus, of course, the prime target audience, the BMW 3 Series. As Jaguar didn't replace the X-Type with a new small car, Jaguar's own XF, the replacement car for the S-Type, has proved a force to be reckoned with as prices of early examples are falling quite dramatically.

The X-Type estate car is particularly useful, either for small businesses, hobbies and DIY (do-it-yourself), or if a sports enthusiast.

2 Cost considerations
– affordable, or a money pit?

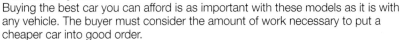

Purchase price

Buying the best car you can afford is as important with these models as it is with any vehicle. The buyer must consider the amount of work necessary to put a cheaper car into good order.

A service history is vital, although these days not necessarily with a franchised dealership. A fully stamped service book from any reputable Jaguar specialist is a good sign, but look for proof of the work actually having been done. Never take an X-Type at face value, as there are hidden issues that could cost a lot of money to rectify.

Servicing

Typical intervals are:

Regular service	10,000 miles
Renew spark plugs	20,000 miles
Renew air filter	30,000 miles
Major service	60,000 miles

Parts price (approximate)

Brake disc kit (front)	●x 65
Brake pad kit (front)	●x 45
Brake disc kit (rear)	●x 50
Brake pad kit (rear)	●x 45
Water pump	●x 65
Thermostat	●x 24
Wheel bearing	●x 30
Control arm	●x 112
Headlamp	●x 235
Headlamp (Xenon)	●x 575
Locking wheel nut kit	●x 65
EGR valve	●x 60
Transmission transfer ass.	●x 880 (surcharge ●x250)
Front wing panel	●x 200

'Buy the best model you can afford' is always the best policy.

Used parts

Inevitably some cars will have found their way to dismantlers, so many parts can now be found. Ensure such parts are tested before purchase (many will come with a guarantee), and beware of model differences when ordering.

A wide choice of used parts can now be found for the X-Type, many of which are guaranteed.

Good points
- Good looks
- Practical size
- Ride and handling
- Smooth engines
- Economy
- Luxurious interior
- Luggage accommodation
- Prestige
- Good support back up

Select the car that most suits your requirements, a pretty standard saloon ...

Bad points
- 'Old Jaguar' styling not to everyone's taste
- Poor quality trim
- Body corrosion
- Electrical maladies
- Low-mileage diesel issues
- Regular maintenance vital (including areas like gearboxes and bushes)

Summary
A very capable, small prestige car that is a good drive. Reasonably economical, but you need to buy the best you can afford, and ensure it has been and will continue to be well maintained, to guard against costly upkeep. Buy the right car for the type of usage to which it will be subjected.

... or a very well equipped estate.

The X-Type was the first Jaguar equipped with all-wheel drive – a major plus point.

4 Relative values
– which model for you?

Models

The body choice is quite simple, with only four-door saloons and five-door estate cars available. The styling remained virtually unchanged until a minor facelift in 2007. However, the model range is quite extensive. A wide choice of engines were available: a 2.0-litre petrol, 2.5-litre petrol, 3.0-litre petrol ,and two diesels of 2.0-litre and 2.2-litre capacity.

There was a proliferation of trim levels, from the original Classic (standard specification), Sport (later Sports Premium), SE (Special Equipment), (later known as Sovereign) to special editions like the Indianapolis, Spirit and XS models. As well as equipment levels and interior trim finishes, exterior styling points identified each model. Taking into account later updates and changes made by previous owners, there is now bound to be a degree of confusion over which model is which!

The vast majority of cars are saloons, as the estates only became available from 2004. By far the largest production came from 2.5 and 3.0-litre petrol-engined cars (virtually twice the number of each, compared to any other versions). The least popular was the 2.0-litre petrol-engined estate car.

In terms of running costs, there won't be a lot to choose between the petrol-engined cars; arguably the larger engines will prove just as fuel efficient as the smaller ones. However, the smaller the engine size, the cheaper the car should be to buy (depending on specification), and this may even affect regular costs like road tax.

The cars' bodies remained virtually identical until the facelift late in 2007 for 2008, which resulted in many relatively minor changes but with a revised front end styling treatment that makes them instantly recognisable. There were several other minor trim changes during the model's life.

Values

As is usually the case, the largest part of a car's perceived value is down to its mileage, condition and specification, regardless of model. In the case of the X-Type, as production finished in 2009 and some were not registered until 2010, some cars may still be in, or have only just left, their original owner's hands. Values of all models are still depreciating, and this trend, although slowing in some cases, is not likely to change in the near future. Ironically in recent times, there has been strong demand for late model estate cars particularly, steadying their prices. Indeed it wasn't so long ago that prices actually started to rise for some models, but that demand and price 'blip' has now faded.

Obviously the older the car the lower the price, but values will vary dramatically according to mileage and history. Top of the range models like the SE, Sovereign and Sport Premium will remain the most expensive to buy because they are also the most sought after. Equipment levels generally, however, will also affect price, so items like the larger alloy wheels, cruise control, satellite navigation, etc will add value to any model, and a lot of these extra cost options may well have been fitted to the lesser models when new.

It's therefore very difficult to evaluate a pricing structure taking account of all this, but given that all things are equal relating to trim and standard equipment levels, the following percentages provide a rough guide.

Model	Percentage
X-Type 2.2-litre diesel estate	100%
X-Type 2.0-litre diesel estate	95%
X-Type 2.2-litre diesel saloon	90%
X-Type 2.0-litre diesel saloon	85%
X-Type 3.0-litre estate	80%
X-Type 2.5-litre estate	80%
X-Type Indianapolis/XS	75%
X-Type 3.0-litre saloon	75%
X-Type 2.5-litre saloon	70%
X-Type 2.0-litre estate	65%
X-Type 2.0-litre saloons	60%

With such a wide choice of models, there is something for everyone at every price. The Sport models differ through their black grille with body-coloured surround, and body-coloured bumper bar blades.

A premium will always be asked for the limited edition or 'special' models like the Indianapolis.

Arden produced a comprehensive range of body and trim kits for the X-Type that were quite expensive, so such equipped models will still hold a premium price.

The later facelift models are most desirable, with better equipment levels and revised exterior styling.

Models like the X and XS fetch a premium because of their specification.

5 Before you view
– be well informed

To avoid a wasted journey, and the disappointment of finding that the car does not match your expectations, it will help if you're very clear about what questions you want to ask before you pick up the telephone. Some of these points might appear basic, but when you're excited about the prospect of buying your dream car, it's amazing how some of the most obvious things slip the mind. Also check the current values of the model you are interested in through car magazines, which give both a price guide (for most models) and auction results.

Where is the car?
Is it going to be worth travelling to the next county/state, or even across a border? A locally advertised car, although it may not sound very interesting, can add to your knowledge for very little effort, so make a visit – it might even be in better condition than expected.

Dealer or private sale
Establish early on if the car is being sold by its owner or by a dealer/ trader. A private owner should have all the history, so don't be afraid to ask detailed questions. A dealer, even a main Jaguar dealer, may have more limited knowledge of a car's history, but should have some documentation. A dealer may offer a warranty/ guarantee (ask for a printed copy) and provide finance.

How is the car being sold? A dealership, independent specialist, general garage, or a private sale?

Cost of collection and delivery
A dealer may well be used to quoting for delivery by car transporter. A private owner may agree to meet you halfway, but only agree to this after you have seen the car at the vendor's address to validate the documentation. Conversely, you could meet halfway and agree the sale, but insist on meeting at the vendor's address for the handover.

View – when and where
It is always preferable to view at the vendor's home or business premises. In the case of a private sale, the car's documentation should tally with the vendor's name and address. Arrange to view only in daylight and avoid a wet day. Most cars look better in poor light or when wet.

Reason for sale
Do make it one of the first questions. Why is the car being sold and how long has it been with the current owner? How many previous owners?

Is the car to original specification, and does it have the equipment level desired? If it has alloy dash trim and you don't want that, don't waste time and money looking at it.

Left-hand drive to right-hand drive
It is highly unlikely that an X-Type will have been converted from left to right-hand drive, but do check the origins of the car. With new cars exported around the world, detail specifications, like lighting, may have applied, so if a car is re-imported, then such detail specifications have to be changed to meet regulations.

Condition (body/chassis/interior/mechanicals)
Ask for an honest appraisal of the car's condition. Ask specifically about some of the check items described in chapter 7.

All original specification
An original equipment car is invariably of higher value than one that has been modified to an individual's taste.

Matching data/legal ownership
Do the VIN, engine numbers and licence plate match the official registration document? Is the owner's name and address recorded in the official registration documents?

Never view a car in rain or under other poor weather conditions. Dampness can hide a multitude of paint and body problems.

For those countries that require an annual test of roadworthiness, does the car have a document showing it complies (an MoT certificate in the UK)?

If a smog/emissions certificate is mandatory, does the car have one?

Does the car carry a current road fund license/licence plate tag?

Does the vendor own the car outright? Money might be owed to a finance company or bank; the car could even be stolen. Several organisations will supply the data on ownership, based on the car's licence plate number, for a fee. Such companies can often also tell you whether the car has been 'written-off' by an insurance company. In the UK these organisations can supply vehicle data:

HPI – 01722 422 422
AA – 0870 600 0836
DVLA – 0870 240 0010
RAC – 0870 533 3660
Other countries will have similar organisations.

Insurance
Check with your existing insurer before setting out, your current policy might not cover you to drive the car if you do purchase it.

How you can pay
A cheque/check will take several days to clear and the seller may prefer to sell to a cash buyer. However, a banker's draft (a cheque issued by a bank) is as good as cash, but safer, so contact your own bank and become familiar with the formalities that are necessary to obtain one.

Buying at auction?
If the intention is to buy at auction see chapter 10 for further advice.

Professional vehicle check (mechanical examination)
There are marque/model specialists who will undertake professional examination of a vehicle on your behalf. Owners clubs will be able to put you in touch with such specialists.

Other organisations that will carry out a general professional check in the UK are –

AA – 0800 085 3007 (motoring organisation with vehicle inspectors)
ABS – 0800 358 5855 (specialist vehicle inspection company)
RAC – 0870 533 3660 (motoring organisation with vehicle inspectors)
Other countries will have similar organisations.

6 Inspection equipment

– these items will really help

This book
Reading glasses (if you need them for close work)
Torch
Probe (a small screwdriver works very well)
Overalls
Mirror on a stick
Digital camera
A friend, preferably a knowledgeable enthusiast

Before you rush out of the door, gather together a few items that will help as you work your way around the car. This book is designed to be your guide at every step, so take it along and use the check boxes to help you assess each area of the car you're interested in. Don't be afraid to let the seller see you using it.

Take your reading glasses if you need them to read documents and make close up inspections.

Such items as a magnet, often used to determine the degree of filler in a body, can be of some use in checking for body repairs.

A torch with fresh batteries will be useful for peering into the wheelarches and under the car.

A digital camera will assist in making a record of what you see, to review later.

A small screwdriver can be used – with care – as a probe, particularly on the underside. With this you should be able to check any areas of corrosion, but be careful – if it's really bad the screwdriver might go right through the metal!

Be prepared to get dirty. Take along a pair of overalls, if you have them. Fixing a mirror at an angle on the end of a stick may seem odd, but you'll probably need it to check the condition of the underside of the car. It will also help you to peer into some of the important crevices. You can also use it, together with the torch, along the underside of the sills and floor. You

Some of the ideal tools to take with you: a good torch, screwdrivers, a mirror, and of course, this guide.

are not just looking for corrosion but also accident damage.

If you have the use of a digital camera, take it along so that later you can study some areas of the car more closely. Take a picture of any part of the car that causes you concern, and seek a friend's opinion.

Ideally, have a friend or knowledgeable enthusiast accompany you: a second opinion is always valuable.

7 Fifteen minute evaluation
– walk away or stay?

Road test

Ensuring you have adequate insurance cover, it is vital you road test any car you are considering purchasing. This should be agreed with the owner prior to viewing, asking him or her, if practical, not to warm the engine, so you can start it from cold.

In the driver's seat, ensure all the usual controls you need work correctly. Seat adjustment, mirrors, etc. Turn on the ignition, start the engine, and allow the car to cycle, dropping the driver's window so you can listen. Upon starting the engine listen for any rattles or other noises from the engine area, or for

A road test over varying conditions is a must before buying a car.

blows from the exhaust system. Engine rattles on start-up could be attributable to worn timing chains, for example. If the engine sounds 'flat' when starting this could be just down to a poor battery.

A quick glance through the rear view mirror should determine any haze or smoke emitting from the exhaust, which should never be a problem with the petrol engines if maintained properly. A small amount of haze from a diesel engine is acceptable at this point. Check the instrument visual read-out for error messages, warning lights, etc. (Disregard the auxiliary gauges except fuel, as they are generally accepted to be 'comfort' instruments and don't provide sufficiently useful information).

The engine should tick over smoothly and quietly. Rev the engine, again listening for unusual noises or hesitation from the throttle, indicating problems to be investigated.

If the car is fitted with a manual gearbox/transmission, push down the clutch and move the gearlever through each gear, feeling for any harshness and trouble engaging any gears. The clutch is relatively light to operate, but if you test drive a couple of examples, you will get a feel for how the clutch pedal should react.

With an automatic transmission model, select Drive. There should be no strong judder as the transmission engages. At this point, check the handbrake is operational, holding the car in Drive, and check that, upon moving off, it releases smoothly.

Moving off, a car with automatic transmission should run smoothly with almost imperceptible gear changes. Earlier cars can suffer from a surge when the car is cold, attributable to a software issue; such cars should have undergone a reflash to rectify. If it's still occurring, it's either because a reflash is needed or, more importantly, because the torque converter needs changing.

With a manual transmission model work your way through all the gears, ensuring they engage smoothly, there is no clutch judder, nor any unusual rattles or vibrations through the car or even the gearlever itself.

With manual transmission models, check through every gear for ease of selection.

With the proliferation of controls, check that everything works. This console doesn't even feature satellite navigation!

Now is the time to put the driver's window up and listen for unacceptable wind noise and for unwarranted knocks and rattles through the car from steering, suspension or the drivetrain. Listen for any 'roaring' noises from the transmission when stationary, and/or any rumblings when on the move, particularly at speed. All these may be attributable to the gearbox transfer unit being worn – a costly item to replace.

Cars with larger alloy wheels and lower profile tyres will give a harder ride, yet there should be no knocks or bumps from the suspension indicating worn bushes or other issues. The brakes should be smooth and progressive. Any judder is normally attributed to warped or corroded discs, which will not be cheap to replace. The steering should be precise with little free play; note any wander.

Large alloy wheels with low profile tyres can create all sorts of noises and vibrations if not maintained properly. This is the probably the first port of call if vibrations are felt on the road test.

Try all the normal operating controls, like air-conditioning and audio system, and check all the auxiliary controls like window motors (if electric) and interior lighting.

Drive the car on varying road surfaces and at different speeds to test for wind noise, wheel balance, and overall smoothness. Ideally a 20-mile round trip is the best way to get a real feel for the car. It's also worth stopping on occasion, switching the engine off and restarting it, again looking for haze or smoke, and listening for rattles or hesitancy in starting, all of which indicate problems to investigate.

Back to the automatic transmission – cycle through the gears to establish the changes take place correctly and smoothly, also trying the Sport mode. The earlier cars suffered from a problem with harsh gear changes, resulting in gearbox failure and replacement. If any harshness is experienced, it is vital to determine why it is still occurring, and whether the car had been properly maintained in the first place, or had any major work done in its earlier life.

With manual transmissions, try stopping and starting on a hill, and also starting in second gear to ensure the clutch is not worn. Wear may be determined not only by the grip of the clutch, but also the smell. As there is no ventilation around the gearbox/clutch/bell housing, a burning or fishy smell coming through into the car will indicate problems.

Try to find a good stretch of straight, clear road to test the cruise control (if fitted), operated from the steering-wheel-mounted controls. Ensure it engages and resumes after braking or accelerating.

Checks back at base

Once you have established from the road test that you want to investigate further, the next stage is to return to base and check other areas.

General condition

In many cases by now these cars may have passed through several owners and have a high mileage, but these models are well suited to extensive use if maintained properly, and one should never be afraid of a high-mileage car if it has been well maintained.

Engine bay

With the engine still running and the handbrake applied, open the bonnet. Look around the engine bay for any apparent fluid leaks and an uneven engine at tickover, and listen for unusual noises. Switch the air-conditioning to full cold and the engine cooling fan should automatically operate, regardless of outside temperature. Ensure it pulls down the temperature promptly by feeling the air coming from the vents inside the car. Check under the bonnet for damaged hoses or clips, and any indications of insufficient or inappropriate maintenance.

A typical X-Type engine bay. Not the cleanest of places to be, but so much easier to check for fluid leaks when dirty.

Even if the air-conditioning is off, the radiator cooling fan is thermostatically controlled, so it should still 'click in' after a period in warm weather if the engine is left running.

The engine bay area doesn't have to be totally clean. If the car has been in regular use, it will have naturally gained a fair amount of road grime, and garages (including dealerships) are often cautious about steam cleaning because of the amount of electronics fitted in modern engine bays.

What condition is the battery in? It lasts a long time and doesn't leak, but once near the end of its life it will affect the car's functionality, and is expensive to replace.

External bodywork

The quality of bodywork preparation by the factory was good, so unless a car has been severely damaged, panel gaps, fit and finish should be excellent. At the front check the nose section, which is particularly vulnerable to stone chips that can penetrate far up the bonnet.

It's worth checking the condition of the headlight units as they can crack and/ or become damp with condensation, and are expensive to replace, particularly if an HID (xenon) lighting system is fitted to the car. If the car is equipped with a headlamp wash system, check that it works.

Check the windscreen for stone chips, pebble rash or other damage, as it is an expensive item to replace, particularly if graduated-tinted or heated.

From the side the lower sill area is merely a plastic covering, and can easily be

A visual check on the bodywork at this stage is vital, and should show up any areas for closer investigation.

damaged by contact with high kerbs, or indeed from the use of a jack.

Both front and rear wheelarches are, as usual, prone to collecting dirt and grime, although with these cars they have rubber covers to protect the area behind. However, the wheelarch lips do collect debris quite easily, which, with rubbing from the rubber covers, can affect the longevity of these panels.

Check for accident damage to the front and rear bumpers, which could be expensive to repair.

Over time the chrome blades on the bumpers (which are actually plastic mouldings) will collect debris and can actually start to crack, with the chrome finish 'lifting.' These were not fitted on the latest facelift for 2007 and later models.

Most X-Types came equipped with alloy wheels, varying in size from 16in to 18in. Many of these wheels are now cheaper to replace than repair, but either way can be an unnecessary cost, and if damaged, are indicative of poor driving (and perhaps maintenance). Check for damage from kerb scuffing, corrosion from hot brake dust, missing centre caps, and even missing or damaged locking wheel nuts. To rectify scuffed rims may be problematic, as many of the X-Type alloys were plastic coated and, over time, water will ingress where the chips have taken place and gradually 'lift' the remaining plastic coating. Centre caps are cheap to replace, but locking wheel nuts have to be purchased in sets, and certainly are not cheap for what they are.

Check the tyres. An X-Type should NEVER be shod with unknown brands, remoulds or tyres over six years old. Pirelli was the recognised factory supplier, and other well-known brands are perfectly acceptable, but are not cheap to replace. Many of the larger tyres fitted to these cars were asymmetric, so must be fitted the right way round.

As a final quick check, it's worth standing back and checking both sides of the car, particularly noting any colour difference between panels indicating earlier damage.

It's important to ensure X-Types have the correct tyres fitted.

Check all the upholstery. Dirt can be easily fixed, damage is more expensive.

Interior

Generally the interiors last very well. Cars, depending on specification, were equipped with either leather seating or forms of cloth. Even those with non-leather upholstery wear well. Usual pointers to watch for are the driver's seat bolster which, with constant rubbing getting in and out of the car, can deteriorate resulting in a new panel having to be let in and suitably dyed.

The majority of cars, except for some of the later facelift models, were fitted with wood veneer trim to the dashboard and door cappings. These areas last exceptionally well but if damaged, it's almost cheaper to replace all the wood than attempt a minor repair!

Some trim items easily show wear and tear. Centre console lids suffer, areas around the glove box lid go discoloured, and some of the solid plastic seat trim can break or become dislodged.

It's worth checking the carpets, particularly on the driver's side, as these are a one-piece design, so will be expensive to replace if there is any damage from shoe heels, etc. The headlining lasts well, but is vulnerable to marks and discolouring, particularly if a smoker has regularly used the car.

Boot

Boot areas also wear well, although the carpet will show marks easily, particularly if the cover for the spare wheel/battery has been regularly removed during maintenance. The estate cars have a much larger load area with a good flat floor that is protected and well covered. However, being an estate, most will have had a variety of uses, from the transit of sports gear, bikes etc, through to usage by traders, antique dealers and many others. Check in detail that the rear compartment is still in good order.

Don't just check the boot area where the luggage goes – remove the cover and check what's underneath.

There should be no signs of exposed wiring or poorly fitted trim, also indicating that someone has been 'there before.' Lift the boot floor spare wheel panel to reveal the spare wheel. Many cars were equipped with a space saver, even though the spare wheel area will accommodate some larger wheel sizes. Is the spare in good condition? Is it correct for the model, both in size and in the alloy wheel design for that car? Are the tools intact, particularly the locking wheel nut adapter? Are all the electrics in place and not tampered with?

There is more storage space under the loading floor of the estate.

Depending on the model and equipment level, the boot may also contain satellite navigation equipment, CD player, Premium Sound amplifier etc, all of which should be undamaged with their covers intact.

The major areas of concern when checking the condition of one of these X-Type models are:
Body/paint condition
Mechanical/electrical integrity
Maintenance history

Bodywork

Although covered in more detail in chapter 9, the bodywork wears very well on these models. The floorpan is part of the overall monocoque structure of the car and is therefore in steel. Not derived from any previous Jaguar models, it carries its parentage from Ford products. Although individual body panels are not a known problem, the biggest area of concern seems to be the inner sill areas, which are hidden behind the plastic over-sills.

The four major key points with the X-Type are: bodywork and paintwork ...

Engines

The Jaguar petrol and diesel engines are long-lived, and some are easily surviving well into 2-300,000 miles with regular and preventive maintenance which is the main issue. Problems experienced with earlier examples of the Jaguar V engines, particularly over matters like timing chain tensioners, water pumps and bore linings on petrol units, and turbo issues on diesels, do not apply to these engines. Turbos can easily cover well over 70,000 miles without any issue.

... followed by the engine (in this case as shown a 2.2-litre diesel model) ...

Transmissions

Gearbox types varied on the X-Type. Originally a 5-speed manual transmission manufactured by Ford or a Jato 5-speed automatic was specified, but later a new 6-speed manual gearbox

... transmission, in the form of the gearbox and transfer units – a known area of concern with X-Types ...

became available on most models, a much improved unit over the older 5-speed gearbox.

Perhaps the only issue (that applies to all the automatic transmissions) is that they are supposedly sealed for life. Because of this, regardless of the car's mileage, often the gearbox will not have had any work carried out on it. But, for longevity, it will need regular oil and filter changes, and it is strongly suggested that such servicing is determined from documentation with the car, or that the work is carried out as soon as possible. This may again affect the price one negotiates for a car.

The 2.0 and 2.2-litre models are front-wheel drive only. All other X-Types have an all wheel drive system (AWD) and there can be issues with the drivetrain, particularly the transfer box aspects which we will discuss in detail in the next chapter. However, similar problems can also apply to the front-wheel drive models.

Suspension, steering & brakes
The X-Type uses a new (to Jaguar) independent suspension system, based on Ford components, which is very reliable in service. The only issue can be the expense of some replacement parts.

The braking system is little different to any other modern all-round-disc equipped car, and doesn't present any special problems.

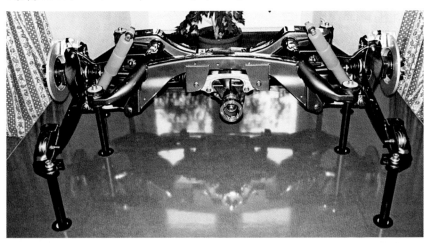

... and suspension, which although relatively straightforward in design, it is still quite complex, as this rear independent setup (with differential, arms, etc) shows.

9 Serious evaluation
– 60 minutes for years of enjoyment

So you've got this far. Now it's time to go for the detail before deciding to part with your hard-earned cash. Read, digest, check against your intended purchase, and then tick the appropriate box (excellent, good, average or poor) and total the points. Be vigilant over the key pointers first highlighted in chapter 8.

Overall stance

Start with the obvious: how does the car sit on the road? These cars naturally sit fractionally lower at the front, so if there is any deviation from this on a flat road surface, suspect some issues. Check the sitting across the whole car, then ask the owner whether any aftermarket suspension changes or small wheels/tyres have been fitted.

Paintwork

There shouldn't have been a need to repaint an X-Type entirely, so look for differences in the colour across panels, under rubbers, and/or overspray, indicating some degree of remedial work. If so, discuss with the owner and confirm why it was carried out, and whether it was done by a reputable company that can handle work on complex modern bodies like these. Under certain light conditions the plastic bumper bar assemblies may appear to be a slightly different shade of colour to the rest of the body – this is normal though. Being factory painted, out-of-sight areas like the inside of wings and under-bonnet areas, may be duller in finish – again, this is normal.

Like most modern cars, used regularly the paintwork may have suffered from stone chips and pebble rash, but if excessive, bear in mind the cost of repainting whole panels and removing or masking trim, all of which can prove expensive.

Areas around the door window frames should be checked for chips and scratches in the gloss black finish, which can be difficult to replicate without ordering replacements.

Bodywork

Panel fit was excellent on these cars, and they are proving particularly long-lived in general service. The gentle curvature of these bodies will easily show up any imperfections, bad panel fit, poor

X-Types should sit pretty evenly front to back.

Look for good fit and finish on all aspects of the bodywork.

Looking across the whole side of the car, particularly from a low angle, should reveal any undulations or non-matching colour.

Look for the official Jaguar identification plate on the B/C post.

The severity of sill corrosion that can take place. The outer plastic sill still looked fine!

On the other side of this car, with the plastic oversill removed, corrosion has started to take hold as can be seen.

Check the rear for scuffs and marks from reverse parking.

Be on the lookout for colour changes along the body, like on the bottom section of this rear door, clearly indicating remedial paintwork.

gaps, dents or bulges where repairs have been carried out.

Starting at the front of the car, is the radiator grille sitting correctly which may indicate some earlier damage/replacement? Recheck the bumper areas for any scuffs or cracks, and the lower areas that may have become damaged from contact with high kerbs. Later models are even more vulnerable here, as the valances extend slightly lower.

Next open the bonnet and check the condition of the inside edges. Do they show any signs of repaint? Also check around the inner wing areas for the same thing, now visible in the engine bay. Does the bonnet open and close cleanly? Certainly check the top of the bonnet for dents, as this is a very curvaceous panel which will be difficult to rectify if damaged in any way.

Moving to the side of the car, start by feeling around the front wheelarch lips, a build up of debris and lack of cleaning around the edges will deter from the original excellent finish and could lead to corrosion.

Check again along the whole side of the car that there are no undulations or minor dents that could prove difficult and costly to rectify. The side rubbing strips can de-bond or get badly scuffed. It's also worth checking for the usual chips around the edges of the doors where they may have been caught against walls and other vehicles. Even touching up can be expensive if done correctly, by an expert.

Next open the doors and check the condition of the paintwork inside, which should be as good as it is externally. Particularly note that the identification sticker is still on the B post passenger (nearside) area. This shows key information about the car and should never be removed – if it appears to have been removed and then refitted, this could be a sign of large amounts of paintwork or bodywork having been carried out. Extensive bodywork repairs here could mean more sinister things (see chapter 11).

Still on the doors area, check for minor corrosion affecting the bottom edges through damp being held inside the panels. There is also a vulnerable area on the A posts (where the front doors hinge) where water can collect.

Although you won't be able to check that easily at this stage, feel around the very bottom of the sill area where the plastic sill covers meet the full metal sills. Corrosion is a known issue here (see 'Underside' section).

At the rear of the car, look for bad scuffs or cracking due to minor impact on the bumper bars. The boot panel shouldn't present any problems unless the top has been damaged with scratches or dents. On the upper face it is not unusual to find minor dents where people have applied pressure to close the boot lid and actually cratered the panel, or the paint has been severely scratched from parcels and luggage.

Remember these cars are built from steel, so it is worth checking everywhere for signs of corrosion. Some of these cars are getting quite old and will have been subjected to all types of weather.

Previous accident damage may well have resulted in the fitting of new panels, but do look for signs of unprofessional (or cheap) workmanship, like overspray, a different paint finish, or signs of filler. If so, consult the seller for more information. Review it all in detail and this can be an ideal negotiating point when buying the car.

Chrome and other trim [4] [3] [2] [1]

Look for the chrome lifting from the bumper bar blades, and check for condensation in the headlight units.

There isn't a lot of chrome on these cars, and most of that is plastic based so shouldn't present any real problems. One area on the pre-facelift models includes the chrome 'blades' at the top, either side of the front and rear bumper bars, mentioned earlier. Over time the chrome bubbles and starts to lift. The only solution is replacement.

Where areas are colour-coordinated to the exterior paint finish, like door handles, mirrors, some radiator surrounds etc, check for paint chips or cracks in the plastic.

The door latches (particularly the driver's door) are known to give problems. Check that all doors lock and unlock and open/close correctly. Replacement costs can be up to ●150 a time, but, in a lot of cases it is just maladjustment. If a fault, then the seller should be able to get it fixed before you agree to buy.

Glass and wipers [4] [3] [2] [1]

Check the front windscreen for pebble rash. It's an expensive item to replace, particularly if heated or graduated tinted. It's a good time to check that the VIN plate (vehicle identification number) is on show in the windscreen. If it isn't, ask the seller why. It is a legal requirement.

It's worth checking the condition of the door window glass, as it can scratch badly from dirt getting into the seals.

Check for the VIN in the windscreen – now a legal requirement.

It has become common practice for owners to have glass tinted to various degrees (known as privacy glass). Something to personal taste, but it must be borne in mind that the tinting of windscreens or front door glass areas can only be done legally up

Beware severely tinted glass – is it legal and well fitted?

to a maximum darkness of 25%. Also, as much of this 'tinting' is done using a plastic film, is it intact, lifting, cracked or peeling? More significantly, if privacy glass is fitted all around and particularly on the rear screen, this can adversely affect signals to the car's audio and sat nav systems.

Check for chips on the edges of glass, and for lock issues with the estate cars.

The wiper blades are quite hefty items and not that cheap to replace, so check their condition. All X-Types are equipped with an auto-wipe facility, which when selected on the steering column stalk should work automatically whenever the windscreen gets wet.

When unlocking the estate car or switching on the ignition, if the rear upper glass area of the tailgate unlocks, this is caused by water ingress into the ribbon switch, and the only solution is replacing the switch.

Interior trim

Interior trim varied according to the model and year. A large number of cars feature leather-faced upholstery, but some had cloth and variants of cloth style upholstery. All had pre-formed one-piece woven carpeting, and in most cases, wood veneered panelling on the dashboard, centre console and doors; on later models, a piano black or dull alloy finish was available.

Interior trim is hard wearing, so start your intensive look with the seating. The driver's seat particularly is where most wear will have taken place, so look at the condition of the leather, especially the bolster area, which is often badly scuffed from trousers with buttons on the back pockets. Look at the overall condition of the

The different styles and finishes of seating in the X-Type, in this case the half cloth/half leather ...

... Alcantara finish, which applied to the Indianapolis model and some later XS and S models.

Leather interior with Sport trim style ...

... compared to leather trim in standard/SE/ Sovereign style.

driver's seat as well – has the cushion stretched or sagged, is there wear in the pile in the case of cloth seating? Also look for damage on the edge of the seat from seatbelt rubbing. Now check the other seats for condition in the same way. In the majority of cases few people will have used the rear compartment, so this should be virtually spotless. In all cases look for splits, tears or severe staining, all of which will be costly to put right.

Sit in the front passenger seat and by moving around quickly and sharply, try to detect any slackness in the seat. This is a problem with the securing of the seat to the floor, and should have been fixed by the Jaguar dealership on an early recall. If not, it needs to be fixed before you buy the car.

Move on to the headlining and sun visors, which wear well. Look for bad scuffs, even tears or discolouring, particularly due to staining from cigarette smoke.

On to the door trims. The only problems here probably relate to bad scuffing or discolouring. Look for bad scratches or knocks in any door wood veneer panelling, usually caused by catching it with a seatbelt buckle for example. Also look for damage to the pocket areas caused by leaking drinks, sticky sweets, or worse.

Minor scuffing can be dealt with easily these days, but small tears and previously repaired sections can lead to more serious costs.

Check to ensure the door panel cards are well secured to the door frame. The plastic clips securing them are prone to breaking if the trim panels have been removed at some time.

The one-piece carpet makes repair difficult without complete replacement, so look for severe wear in the driver's and passenger's footwell.

The demisting vents on the top of the dashboard roll gave problems on the earlier cars, popping out of position in hot weather as the dash expanded. This was resolved by changing the securing buttons on the ends of the vents. On early cars there was no button on the driver's side. It was the job of the air-conditioning sun-load sensor to hold the vent in. This was removed, and the same securing button as used on the passenger side was fitted. The button should be colour coded the same as the vent, but if the button looks blue, this is a sun-load sensor, so the vent may still be insecure.

It is worth checking the nearside footwell carpets for damp. Early cars had an issue with water ingress

Door trim styles vary, but look out for bad scuffs, discolouring of trim, and door cards not properly secured to the doors.

Be sure to check out the carpet, particularly on the driver's side. Expensive to replace, and most X-Types had overmats – are they still there, and what is underneath them?

into the vehicle via the air intake for the heater. Water would get past the pollen filter and run into the passenger's foot area, more so if the vehicle was left parked on a slope with the front end high. Dealers were told to fit a water shield to the pollen filter housing, obstructing the rain water and stopping the ingress. Even where these shields have been fitted, however, it is not unknown for them to be damaged by garages when changing the pollen filter.

Check out the rear seating. There were reports of ink stains from the coding on the underside of the leather hides, working its way through to the upper surface; this should have been cured under warranty.

Instrumentation and electrics

It's important to check that everything electrical works on these cars. There are, for example, numerous sensors at the front of the car that can be easily damaged and, if so, create error messages on the dashboard. All such messages should be checked out; consider any problems here to be potentially expensive as there are so many sensors around the car and they all play an important part in matters as diverse as temperature monitoring, cruise control modules, smog control, diesel particulate filters and much more.

Start by checking the electrics for both front seats, as all models had some form of electrical adjustment, including the headrests. Also check for the memory functions (which will vary from driver's seat only to both front seats, depending on specification). Some cars had heating elements in the seating as well – check they function.

The main instrument pack and dashboard mounted switch layout are the same for all models, save for some calibration and minor identification in the rev counter according to engine. Look for any error messages that show up in the green digital read-out, usually accompanied by an orange or red warning light. Red indicates an immediate, important issue to be addressed, orange warns of impending issues that must be checked as soon as possible. The majority of messages can be cleared only by connecting to diagnostic equipment, which will provide a more accurate assessment as to what has triggered the warning. Any such problem areas should be addressed by the seller before you buy.

An air bag light is situated on the dashboard passenger side, which many refer to as a 'warning' light. This is not so – it's merely a means of identifying that a passenger is not of sufficient mass to activate

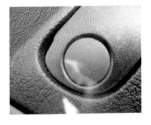

The air vent button should be the same colour as the vent; if not, it is a sensor, and the vents haven't been adapted by Jaguar.

the air bag (ie with a child seat installed). If, however, this light is on when nobody is sitting in that seat or when an adult is, then there is a problem that must be identified, and could result in an MoT failure.

Check all the other controls. Interior roof lighting, courtesy light operation, electrically operated window lifts, door mirror adjustment, electric steering wheel adjustment, horns, wiper wash/wipe, headlamp flashers, and don't forget the original extra-cost accessories if fitted, like a windscreen heater element, sunroof, etc.

Sound system equipment varied, but all models were operated by the switchpack on the centre console with accompanying controls on the steering column. The centre console features either a single-slot cassette or CD insert, or switchgear for the CD auto-changer. The console has further switches and TFT read-out or a multi-function large format TFT screen. The different styles of centre console area can be seen from the

The boot/rear compartment of estate models, carries auxiliary equipment like the CD stacker unit and satellite navigational control unit, where fitted.

A visual readout will help you determine if the car has phone or voice activation installed.

... and here with full satellite navigation and on-screen controls.

accompanying pictures. Other functions relating to air-conditioning, telephone, etc. are also operated from this console area. Where a CD stacker system is fitted, the unit will be in the boot/rear compartment area. It was also possible to have a TV/DVD tuner fitted, also with its functions on the centre console display (only where a TFT screen is fitted). It's worth running through all the on-screen functions to determine everything works.

In the case of television receivers fitted to these models, they are all pre-digital so with no analogue signal available, there will be no effective reception. Jaguar do not supply a modification to convert these systems so this is another good negotiating point; why pay for something you will not be able to use?

Steering wheel buttons include cruise control features on the right-hand side. Check that it works and, in the case of 2.2-litre diesel models, that the Jaguar modifications have been carried out in view of the major problem experienced with it not disconnecting.

Finally on the dashboard/centre console area, check the condition of the trim finish. Wood veneer can crack and scratch, piano black finishes are particularly prone to scratching (and collecting static), and the alloy finish can also mark and discolour.

Many X-Types are also equipped with an integrated satellite navigation system, controlled from the centre console and the same TFT screen used for other features. The system is controlled from a DVD unit in the boot/rear compartment. Check that this works, although bear in mind that the operating disk may not be up-to-date. The latest known update is for 2011, and is available from Jaguar Cars dealerships by special order, but it will cost several hundred pounds so is a good negotiating point when buying. Alternatively, there are some after-market copies around at much cheaper prices, BUT be careful: a faulty copy or inappropriate disk could 'write off' the equipment's software.

A few cars have a voice activation system installed, enabling the driver to make various changes, for example to the media system or air-conditioning settings, by voice control, using an activation switch on the left-hand side of the steering wheel. Apart from the original owners, some subsequent owners do not even know if this is fitted! Press the lower button on the left-hand side of the steering wheel – if it mutes the sound system, then there is no voice activation fitted. If it displays "listening" in the centre console, then it is operational and awaiting a command. The system will not be programmed to your voice, so may not respond correctly, but at least you know it is operational.

Another thing not always known is that all these cars are fitted with phone buttons in either the touch screen or standard radio. The very early cars had a GSM fixed phone, which used a handset in the centre armrest. Is it still there and if so, does it work? Later cars were equipped with a Bluetooth connection. By pressing the phone button on the radio or the hard key on the side of a touch screen, this will tell if a phone is fitted or not. If the vehicle displays the message "No Phone" or "No Phone Fitted", the vehicle does not have a phone system. However if it displays "Handset in Use" or just "Handset," the vehicle has a phone but it needs to be paired via Bluetooth.

All these X-Types are fitted with multi-air bags that don't require any maintenance. However, if an air bag warning light comes on, this is an automatic MoT failure.

Check areas like the external mounted parking sensors, which were standard on later models, front and rear. Recheck that cruise control is working. Many owners don't use it, but you should still check.

A major issue affecting the X-Type 2.2-litre diesel models fitted with cruise control (2006 to 2010 models) was identified. The cruise either would not engage, with an accompanying message on the dashboard "Cruise Not Available," or it engaged but would NOT disengage. This was a serious issue, and all cars were recalled to the Jaguar dealerships for rectification. You need to check that the recall was effected.

One of the most alarming issues that can occur whilst driving the car is the whole dashboard set of lights and warnings coming on like a Christmas tree! This is usually a blip caused by a temporary fall-off in communications in the car. Stopping, turning the engine off, and restarting will usually reset everything without issue. If, of course, it continues, this is where specialist help is required, and you may wish to walk away from the car or ensure the seller gets this rectified before you consider buying!

Lighting

4 3 2 1

Check all the lights to ensure they are working, looking particularly at the headlight units as they collect condensation and will eventually need replacing. In the case of HID (xenon) units, check they operate correctly as they can be costly to repair and replace. Most likely problems come from failure, but bear in mind this isn't a matter of a simple bulb replacement, but more likely a burner unit.

Check the auxiliary driving lights set into the front bumper are not damaged, as they suffer badly from stone chips and water ingress. The car is also equipped with an auto-lighting facility triggered by a sensor, so by selecting 'auto' on the car's lighting switch, the lights should automatically come on and go out when necessary, like on entering and leaving a tunnel.

All X-Type exhausts are of stainless steel construction (although not necessarily of the finest stainless quality) and present no real problems. Some sellers may have fitted aftermarket systems, so it's worth checking for excessive noise levels that take away from the general refinement of the car, or for poorly fitted systems. As most of the exhaust tailpipes are chrome finish (except for some diesels), it is always a sign of care by previous owners if these are clean and polished rather than left to the elements, going rusty.

Damaged alloys will cost you money.

Standard equipment wheels were alloy on all models with a proliferation of different styles spread over 16in, 17in or 18in diameter. The important thing is to check they all match, not just in style but also in size! Such wheels are vulnerable to damage from kerbing as mentioned earlier, so check the overall condition. If badly damaged, this is a good negotiating point. Not only are they costly to repair or replace, but, in the case of the former, one has to ensure they are still 'round.' Alloy wheels suffer badly from misshaping, and once this has happened, it becomes increasingly difficult to get wheels and tyres balanced to avoid vibration in the car. This can certainly be another cause of any imbalance noted during the road test. Also it is quite common for the inner surfaces of these alloys wheels to bend and even crack, so give them a thorough going-over at this point.

The locking wheel nut adapter doesn't last long, and a new one comes with a new set of nuts (expensive!)

Wheel nuts can create problems through water ingresses between the nuts and wheels, and can cause corrosion so that when they are undone, the nuts crack and break off. Also look for bruised nuts, which could indicate previous problems in trying to remove them. The locking key supplied in the tool kit is not a long-lived item, so check that.

It is worth checking the handbook to determine the correct tyres for the particular model, to ensure that even if the original Pirelli equipment is not fitted, a reputable brand and correct size is. Good tyres are expensive and wear rate is generally not that good, particularly on the front wheels; a problem with front-wheel and all-wheel drive cars in general. Ensure the tread is sufficiently good and that the wheels are correctly balanced. Any uneven tyre wear deserves wider investigation. It is quite common to find that these cars are not tracked correctly.

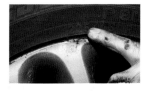

Check the size and condition of the tyres with those identified in the handbook.

Bonnet and boot

The boot lid has an electrically controlled lock, so it shouldn't be necessary to slam it shut. The boot lid can either by released by the push-button on the rear panel or from the keyfob.

The estate car roofs got damaged on the earlier models, because the spoiler caught it when the door was opened. Jaguar should have fixed this on all cars by now.

Rear chrome finishers also caused problems, rubbing against the paint and causing corrosion.

The estate car rear door can show the lock problem (mentioned earlier), but remember to check the separate glass top section, as it opens and closes independently of the bottom half, making sure it is not scratched, cracked, or chipped. There was also an issue with the rear tailgate spoiler catching the roof panel when opened. A recall from Jaguar moved the spoiler slightly to prevent it catching. Apparently, some estates may not have had this procedure carried out, so check it. Some obvious signs are the spoiler still catching, or, even if the rectification was carried out, any marks or dents in the roof that were not addressed at the time.

Finally, on the pre-facelift models, a common problem was the chrome finish on the boot lid/estate car door. With its sharp edges it cuts its way through the paintwork, and with ingress of damp and water over a period, causes corrosion. Anyone identifying this problem to a Jaguar dealership should have had the finisher removed, the panel repainted, and the finisher replaced with padded washers to prevent a reoccurrence; check this area for the problem.

Underside

The underside of an X-Type is protected by rubberised panels screwed to the floorpan and even the engine bay. They should be intact and undamaged. It is vital these are fitted for cleanliness, tidiness, stabilising the aerodynamics of the car, and, because they are heavily insulated, particularly for diesel models, acting as sound deaderners. You can't see a lot of the underside without actually removing them, which may prove difficult unless the owner allows the car to be inspected where access to a ramp is possible. If this is not possible or practical, as detailed a look as possible will give you some indication of any areas of concern, like damage or leaking fluids.

What the average X-Type will look like underneath. Removing the protective panel underneath the engine can reveal a lot.

Damage can be caused to the trailing arm when someone tries to jack up the car in the wrong position.

Typical corrosion areas under the X-Type.

This car has been grounded, or at the very least caught a few kerbs, as the rubber deflector is badly frayed under the front valance.

If it is possible to unbolt these panels, then an overall view of the complete underside can be made. Brake pipe lines run the length of the car (look for corrosion), and a general assessment of the floorpan and mechanics, mainly from a damage rather than corrosion perspective, should be done. In general terms the cars are holding up remarkably well, with the only specifically known problem area being the inner sills. Many areas of the suspension etc will show surface rust by now; in most cases this is not terminal, but should be addressed if you buy the car to keep. Built from conventional steel, they are not as well protected as other visible parts, and are hidden from view by the plastic over-sills on the outside. Damp and debris can build up and these corrode quite easily.

Miscellaneous checks

Are there two sets of keys and remote control fobs with the car? There were when new. Check that both fobs work and that all the keys are present, as these will be costly to replace. If either of the fobs don't work, they will either require new batteries (not too expensive) or, particularly if batteries have been removed for any length of time, reprogramming by a garage with Jaguar's diagnostic equipment (more expensive).

It's also worth checking that there is a valid security code for the sound system. If the battery is disconnected, the system will require a code to be entered. If you don't have that code, it will cost you to get one through Jaguar.

There should be two sets of keys and both fobs should work, otherwise they may have to be reprogrammed.

It's worth a final check to ensure all the tools that were supplied with the new car are still there, particularly the wheel nut locking tool, the jack, wheelbrace. Also all the original handbooks and manuals, of which there were several (dependent on specification).

Engine bay

Given the checks you made in the fifteen minute evaluation, now look in more detail at areas like the overall condition of everything under the bonnet. Don't expect everything to be clean, as most garages don't like using pressure washers because

A typical example of a non-specialist working on these complex cars – an electrical 'bodge!'

It only takes a few clips to remove the cover to the air cleaner. A good clean filter (left) can say a lot about car maintenance: compare it with the one on the right, from an ill-maintained engine.

of the amount of electronics now built into the cars. Dust and dirt can certainly help in showing up fluid leaks and other problems. Look for hoses in poor condition, cable ties, or other areas that may indicate that some areas and/or components have been interfered with. Plastic clips on the rear panel below the scuttle are prone to breaking if this area has been disturbed. The panel itself may be damaged.

Engine

The engines are known for their reliability, and should be able to sustain 10,000 miles between services without the addition of any fluids. It is, however worth checking the condition of the oil on the engine oil dipstick; if the oil looks black and thick, this is a sure sign that the car has not been regularly serviced. Check this with the service book and other data, and discuss with the owner.

Most of the engine is covered by plastic panelling, which doesn't take much to remove, but get permission from the seller. It's worth taking it off for a close look at what is underneath.

These cars are not ideal for DIY enthusiasts, so apart from engine oil, filter and sparkplug changes, there isn't much that most owners can do to maintain them unless you have good experience, the right tools and a degree of expertise in modern engineering and electronics. Therefore check the stamps on the service book and, if possible, compare them with any other paperwork to confirm what has been done and by whom. It is vital these engines are regularly serviced as they do not respond well to long-term use without regular oil changes.

Common problems, applicable to any car these days, relate to sensors failing. This can cause a range

With an engine cover removed, you gain access to much of the engine, to check for apparent leaks and other signs of poor maintenance.

Although there are no cam belts, it is important to check the engine drive belts, which are a little difficult to see.

of symptoms, some accompanied by messages on the dashboard, others just by erratic running, difficult starting, poor fuel consumption, etc: all of which are best diagnosed with specialist equipment. Example symptoms might be caused, for example, by not having the spark plugs changed at the correct interval which could result in fault codes that don't relate to the plugs at all, such is the complexity of modern electronics.

Some 2.5-litre and 3.0-litre V6 petrol engines are known for producing a slight droning noise at around 2600rpm, which Jaguar put down to an engine imbalance. Not a problem, but if it becomes intrusive it can be fixed by replacing the top engine mount, which is now weighted to counteract the imbalance – but this is at a cost of several hundred pounds!

A final point is that very occasionally, under harsh acceleration a white haze comes from the exhaust system. This is merely a build-up of condensation, which under acceleration is pushed up to meet the exhaust gases, creating the haze.

With diesel engines there are some important things to note. Low mileage diesel engines tend to carry more soot, which can lead to several issues, sometimes major. In extreme cases, turbo damage and/or EGR failure or the DPF can cause issues. The bottom line here is that in most cases, low mileage creates most of the problems associated with diesel engines.

An EGR (exhaust gas recirculation) valve failure is quite common, but a prospective buyer is not going to be able to identify the cause of a problem, other than to see a warning on the dashboard readout which may just say "Consult Handbook." However, an indication that this is the actual problem may be found in a slight hissing sound when the accelerator is depressed. Often this can be caused by a split hose to the EGR valve, rather than the valve itself, which is much simpler to replace. It's a large rubber hose connecting the EGR valve to the intercooler on diesel engines. It is difficult to locate, and although the parts are not expensive to replace, it should be dealt with before you buy the car.

The biggest single area of concern with low mileage diesels is the DPF (diesel particulate filter). Not all X-Type diesels have a DPF fitted, so for ease of identification, open the bonnet, look down the back of the engine, behind the turbo and before the bulkhead, and there is what looks like a large catalyst. If this has a heat sensor (looking like an oxygen sensor) with a blue wire coming from it, this shows that the car does have a DPF. Also, if the car has a service light fitted to the instrument pack, it must have a DPF fitted.

The filter is there as part of the overall emissions system, to remove a high proportion of the harmful carbon microspheres (or soot) before it leaves the exhaust. It filters the particles and stores them until they are burnt away, emptying the filter. This is done by sending fuel down the exhaust to the filter, which is then ignited. This creates a high temperature, and heat can be felt generated from underneath the car. If cars are run for very short mileages at low speeds, the particles build up to an unacceptable level, which will produce a warning light on the dashboard, strong smells from underneath the car, and, in the worst case scenario, can cause a fire. A knock-on effect of all this is that the fuel goes back into the engine oil, raising the overall oil level, causing fuel wash and accelerated engine wear. In the worst cases, the engine will run on its own oil with ultimately incredible damage.

Note therefore any smell and excessive heat generated from beneath the car, and check the engine oil to see if it is above the full level mark. Finally, check the computer read-out on the dashboard for fuel consumption. If it shows a very low figure, then it is indicative of a car used on very short journeys.

Usually, running the car on the motorway for a while at at speeds that consume over 45mpg will cure this. Otherwise it is a matter for the Jaguar dealership or independent specialist to rectify.

With the 2.0-litre diesel engines there are instances of severe vibration when starting and warming up. This usually means the engine requires a 'reflash' of its software, which has to be done with Jaguar diagnostic equipment.

The turbos are long lived. However, contamination by putting petrol into a diesel engine can mean a complete replacement of the high pressure system, which can cost several thousand pounds – be warned, and check that history!

Lastly, all the engines are chain driven, so the common issue of cambelt changes do not apply to these cars.

Cooling system   4   3   2   1

The cooling systems are very reliable, and the most likely cause of any problems is a build-up of debris against the front of the radiator core, preventing airflow. In most cases this can be rectified by removing the front grille and using a high-pressure washer. With high-mileage cars, it is recommended you drain the cooling system, flush the radiator and its core extensively, and refill with the correct mix of antifreeze.

Carry out a further test of the car's heating system. If you find that one side is hot and the other is running cold (given correct adjustment of the centre console temperature settings), this can be put down to a failing heater matrix which is expensive to replace because the dashboard has to be stripped down to access it.

The air-conditioning system should be serviced every two years, so evidence of this should be found in the paperwork with the car.

Fuel system   4   3   2   1

All models – petrol and diesel – have a multi-point fuel-injection system that is exceptionally reliable, and again, because of its complexity, needs a diagnostic system to analyse any issues relating to it.

Transmission/drivetrain   4   3   2   1

The choice of transmission was down to manual gearboxes (dependent on model) or automatics. The manual transmissions are very reliable indeed, and the clutches should last well into the 100,000 mile bracket with careful driving (although there have been cases of earlier failure where cars have towed a lot). It is vital that, if oil changes have been made, the correct type of fluid has been used. Look for evidence of this in the paper work.

The automatic transmissions are also very reliable and smooth in operation. These modern units have their own 'memory,' which will adapt to suit the regular driver of the car in the way he/she uses the accelerator and brakes. With a new driver, this can take some time to adjust to a different driving style.

Having said that, all gear changes should be exceptionally smooth, almost imperceptible when the gearbox is not set to the 'Sport' mode. Even then gear

Rubber driveshaft boots should be checked for cracking and water ingress.

changes should not be harsh. If there are any signs of sluggish or harsh changes, this needs investigating.

These automatic transmissions are described as "sealed for life," but in reality they need regular oil and filter changes, which is not particularly a DIY job because gearbox temperatures have to be maintained and special equipment is required to replace the oil. If buying a car with over 60,000 miles on the clock, it is worth asking the owner if an oil/filter change has been done. If not, it is one of the first service operations you should have done after purchase. Very low mileage cars can run for up to five years, but then should certainly have their gearbox oil changed.

It is certainly not unknown for X-Types to suffer from some form of drivetrain vibration. Disregarding usual problems of wheel balance, other forms of vibration can show themselves through the seats, and can disappear when the car isn't under hard load. The only true way to identify these issues is to have the car put onto Jaguar's diagnostic equipment, which has a vibration analyser.

Transmission transfer boxes are a regular problem with X-Types. First, check for any oil leaks coming from the rear of the engine area underneath the car. Second, when starting the engine, listen for a howling noise coming from the transmission. When driving at a reasonable speed also listen for a whining noise, all of which can indicate transfer box problems. This is a costly item to replace – up to several thousand !

Brakes and steering

Again the brakes and steering are not only very reliable, but also particularly good. The rack and pinion steering system is without problem, and, given good driving conditions, will last over 200,000 miles without issues.

The all-round ventilated disc brakes are excellent. If the brakes pull to one side on application, or you feel a judder through the pedal, it is a sure sign that the discs are warped and near the end of their life. Even if there isn't an opportunity to remove the road wheels, the condition of the discs can be checked, in many cases

Even if you can't access the underside or the brakes from the inside of the wheels, a good view can be had through the alloy wheels, in this case revealing a lot of corrosion on the caliper and disc.

The front suspension and steering system of the X-Type. Problems with slight groans from the steering can usually be fixed at little cost, but check the rack for fluid leaks.

The brake and suspension system on the X-Type are conventional so the usual problems of bushes, brake pads and discs and dampers need to be considered.

by looking through the alloy wheels. Corrosion around the edges and grooves in the disc face are sure signs that they need replacing.

The rear brakes are known to be prone to a 'moaning' (ghostly!) noise when negotiating corners. This was caused by a disc moving over slightly to touch the brake pad. Jaguar's original 'fix' was to chamfer the pads, and later pads were manufactured with this chamfer to prevent the problem. However, even today many cars still have old stock pads fitted, or indeed repro pads (neither have the chamfer), and in severe circumstances, even with chamfered pads, the noise can reoccur, in which case new discs are probably required.

It is not unknown for the steering to squeak as you turn the steering wheel. This is down to poor lubrication of a seal, and the Jaguar 'fix' was putting additive in the power steering fluid. If the additive has been used,

Brake lines should be checked for corrosion.

there should be a white sticker on the power steering reservoir under the bonnet, carrying a CTS part number. If there is and the noise is still there, the additive cannot be re-added, so it is most likely that a new steering rack may be required.

Suspension

The cars run on conventional coil springs with shock absorbers, which are very reliable in service.

It is difficult to determine when replacements parts are required, as this is not necessarily down to mileage only, but also to the type of driving the car is subjected to. It is not unusual to find that shock absorbers need replacing after 60-70,000 miles, and bushes at around the same time. If any items need replacing, it will be because of a harsh ride, the vehicle sitting to one side, or noises coming from the suspension under load.

There are quite a number of bushes on the suspension system of these cars,

A typical corroded damper and disintegrating bush.

There are many bushes to regularly maintain on the X-Type. Note the severity of the surface corrosion in this instance.

all of which will wear over time and mileage, causing knocking noises, handling issues, and, of course, tyre wear, which is the most common sign of problems. At the front the top arms and lower ball joints all can have play and create knocking noises, but are easily replaceable. Other common problems are track control arm bushes and trailing arm bushes wearing. In the case of the trailing arms, it is not unknown for people to jack up the rear of the car under these arms, instead of in the correct area, which bends the arms making replacement necessary. A quick check underneath can identify this.

Wheel bearings can be a common problem because of the overall weight of the car, plus the fitting of larger wheels and tyres. The best way to check for wear in the bearings is to jack up the car, grab each wheel in turn, and rock them back and forth.

Evaluation procedure
Add up the total points.
Score: 76 = excellent; 57 = good; 38 = average; 19 = poor. Cars scoring over 53 will be completely usable and will require only maintenance and care to preserve condition. Cars scoring between 19 and 39 will require some serious work (at much the same cost regardless of score). Cars scoring between 40 and 52 will require very careful assessment of the necessary repair/restoration costs in order to arrive at a realistic value.

10 Auctions
– sold! Another way to buy your dream

Auctions are a good source of X-Type models providing you take sufficient care over your intending purchase.

Auction pros & cons
Pros: Prices will usually be lower than those of dealers or private sellers and you might grab a real bargain on the day. Auctioneers have usually established clear title with the seller. At the venue you can usually examine documentation relating to the vehicle.

Cons: You have to rely on a sketchy catalogue description of condition and history. The opportunity to inspect is limited and you cannot drive the car. Auction cars are often a little below par and may require some work. It's easy to overbid. There will usually be a buyer's premium to pay in addition to the auction hammer price.

Which auction?
Auctions by established auctioneers are advertised in car magazines and on the auction houses' websites. A catalogue, or a simple printed list of the lots for auctions might only be available a day or two ahead, though often lots are listed and pictured on auctioneers' websites much earlier. Contact the auction company to ask if previous auction selling prices are available as this is useful information (details of past sales are often available on websites).

Catalogue, entry fee and payment details
When you purchase the catalogue of the vehicles in the auction, it often acts as a ticket allowing two people to attend the viewing days and the auction. Catalogue details tend to be comparatively brief, but will include information such as 'one owner from new, low mileage, full service history', etc. It will also usually show a guide price to give you some idea of what to expect to pay and will tell you what is charged as a 'Buyer's premium'. The catalogue will also contain details of acceptable forms of payment. At the fall of the hammer an immediate deposit is usually required, the balance payable within 24 hours. If the plan is to pay by cash there may be a cash limit. Some auctions will accept payment by debit card. Sometimes credit or charge cards are acceptable, but will often incur an extra charge. A bank draft or bank transfer will have to be arranged in advance with your own bank as well as with the auction house. No car will be released before all payments are cleared. If delays occur in payment transfers then storage costs can accrue.

Buyer's premium
A buyer's premium will be added to the hammer price: don't forget this in your calculations. It is not usual for there to be a further state tax or local tax on the purchase price and/or on the buyer's premium.

Viewing
In some instances it's possible to view on the day, or days before, as well as in

the hours prior to, the auction. There are auction officials available who are willing to help out by opening engine and luggage compartments and to allow you to inspect the interior. While the officials may start the engine for you, a test drive is out of the question. Crawling under and around the car as much as you want is permitted, but you can't suggest that the car you are interested in be jacked up, or attempt to do the job yourself. You can also ask to see any documentation available.

Bidding

Before you take part in the auction, decide your maximum bid – and stick to it!

It may take a while for the auctioneer to reach the lot you are interested in, so use that time to observe how other bidders behave. When it's the turn of your car, attract the auctioneer's attention and make an early bid. The auctioneer will then look to you for a reaction every time another bid is made, usually the bids will be in fixed increments until the bidding slows, when smaller increments will often be accepted before the hammer falls. If you want to withdraw from the bidding, make sure the auctioneer understands your intentions – a vigorous shake of the head when he or she looks to you for the next bid should do the trick!

If buying at auction, set yourself a financial limit before you start bidding.

Assuming that you are the successful bidder, the auctioneer will note your card or paddle number, and from that moment on you will be responsible for the vehicle.

If the car is unsold, either because it failed to reach the reserve or because there was little interest, it may be possible to negotiate with the owner, via the auctioneers, after the sale is over.

Successful bid

There are two more items to think about. How to get the car home, and insurance. If you can't drive the car, your own or a hired trailer is one way, another is to have the vehicle shipped using the facilities of a local company. The auction house will also have details of companies specialising in the transfer of cars.

Insurance for immediate cover can usually be purchased on site, but it may be more cost-effective to make arrangements with your own insurance company in advance, and then call to confirm the full details.

eBay & other online auctions?

eBay and other online auctions could land you a car at a bargain price, though you'd be foolhardy to bid without examining the car first, something most vendors encourage. A useful feature of eBay is that the geographical location of the car is shown, so you can narrow your choices to those within a realistic radius of home. Be prepared to be outbid in the last few moments of the auction. Remember, your bid is binding and that it will be very, very difficult to get restitution in the case of a crooked vendor fleecing you – caveat emptor!

Be aware that some cars offered for sale in online auctions are 'ghost' cars. Don't part with any cash without being sure that the vehicle does actually exist and is as described (usually pre-bidding inspection is possible).

Auctioneers

Barrett-Jackson www.barrett-jackson.com
Bonhams www.bonhams.com
British Car Auctions BCA) www.bca-europe.com or www.british-car-auctions.co.uk
Cheffins www.cheffins.co.uk
Christies www.christies.com
Coys www.coys.co.uk
eBay www.eBay.com
RM www.rmauctions.com
Shannons www.shannons.com.au
Silver www.silverauctions.com

There can be several examples at a single auction, so check them all before you start bidding.

11 Paperwork
– correct documentation is essential!

Classic, collector and prestige cars usually come with a large portfolio of paperwork accumulated and passed on by a succession of proud owners. This documentation represents the real history of the car, and from it can be deduced the level of care the car has received, how much it's been used, which specialists have worked on it, and the dates of major repairs and restorations. All of this information will be priceless to you as the new owner, so be very wary of cars with little paperwork to support their claimed history.

Registration documents
All countries/states have some form of registration for private vehicles whether it's like the American 'pink slip' system or the British 'log book' system.

It is essential to check that the registration document is genuine, that it relates to the car in question, and that all the vehicle's details are correctly recorded, including VIN and engine numbers (if these are shown). If you are buying from the previous owner, his or her name and address will be recorded in the document: this will not be the case if you are buying from a dealer.

In the UK, the current (Euro-aligned) registration document is named 'V5C' and the front is now principally red. Inside sections relate to the car specification, with a section to advise the DVLA in the UK of the details of a new owner when the car is sold. A small section in yellow deals with selling the car within the motor trade.

In the UK the DVLA will provide details of earlier keepers of the vehicle upon payment of a small fee, and much can be learned in this way.

If the car has a foreign registration there may be expensive and time-consuming formalities to complete.

Do you really want the hassle?

Roadworthiness certificate
Most country/state administrations require that vehicles are regularly tested to prove that they are safe to use on the public highway and do not produce excessive emissions. In the UK that test (the 'MoT') is carried out at approved testing stations, for a fee. In the USA the requirement varies, but most states insist on an emissions test every two years as a minimum, while the police are charged with pulling over unsafe-looking vehicles.

In the UK the test is required on an annual basis once a vehicle becomes three years old. Of particular relevance for older cars is that the certificate issued includes the mileage reading recorded at the test date and, therefore, becomes an independent record of that car's history. Ask the seller if previous certificates are available. Without an MoT the vehicle should be trailered to its new home, unless you insist that a valid MoT is part of the deal. (Not such a bad idea this, as at least you will know the car was roadworthy on the day it was tested and you don't need to wait for the old certificate to expire before having the test done.)

Road licence
The administration of every country/state charges some kind of tax for the use of its

road system, the actual form of the 'road licence' and, how it is displayed, varying enormously country to country and state to state.

Whatever the form of the 'road licence', it must relate to the vehicle carrying it and must be present and valid if the car is to be driven on the public highway legally. The value of the license will depend on the length of time it will continue to be valid.

In the UK if a car is untaxed because it has not been used for a period of time, the owner has to inform the licencing authorities, otherwise the vehicle's date-related registration number will be lost and there will be a painful amount of paperwork to get it re-registered.

Certificates of authenticity
For many makes of car it is possible to get a certificate proving the age and authenticity (e.g. engine and VIN numbers, paint colour and trim) of a particular vehicle. These are called Heritage Certificates, and in the case of the XJ, depending on the age of the car, it may be possible to acquire one from Jaguar Heritage in Coventry, UK. If the car comes with one of these it is a definite bonus. If you want to obtain one, contact the Trust via www.jaguarheritage.com

Valuation certificate
Even though these X-types are still quite modern, the vendor may have a recent valuation certificate, or letter signed by a recognised expert stating how much he, or she, believes the particular car to be worth (such documents, together with photos, are usually needed to get 'agreed value' insurance). Generally such documents should act only as confirmation of your own assessment of the car, rather than a guarantee of value ,as the expert has probably not seen the car in the flesh. The easiest way to find out how to obtain a formal valuation is to contact the owners' club.

Service history
Naturally, few, if any of these cars will have been maintained by the DIY mechanic, so look for dealer stamps, or specialist garage receipts, all of which will score most points in the value stakes. However, anything helps in the great authenticity game – items like the original bill of sale, handbook, parts invoices and repair bills add to the story and character of the car. Even a brochure from the year of the car's manufacture is a useful document, and something that you could well have to search hard to locate in future years.

If the seller claims to have carried out regular servicing, ask what work was completed, when, and seek some evidence of it being carried out. Your assessment of the car's overall condition should tell you whether the seller's claims are genuine.

Restoration photographs
None of these cars are old enough or will have suffered sufficiently to warrant any restoration work. However, some refurbishment may have been carried out, particularly to areas like paintwork. If the seller tells you that any work has been carried out, over the normal maintenance mentioned, then expect to be shown a series of communications, receipts, or even photographs taken while the work was under way. Pictures taken at various stages, and from various angles, should help you gauge the thoroughness of the work. If you buy the car, ask if you can have all such information, as this forms an important part of the vehicle's history. It's

surprising how many sellers are happy to part with their car and accept your cash, but want to hang on to any other documentation! In this event, you may be able to persuade the vendor to get a set of copies made.

Other important paperwork
These are sophisticated cars and may be equipped with a range of special, costly extras like voice activation, satellite navigation, etc. All these had their own operating handbooks, so it is worth ensuring you get ALL the relevant manuals and handbooks that should have accompanied the car when new.

A lot of paperwork comes with modern Jaguars, so ensure it's all there.

Service history is vital to confirm work that has been carried out on the car.

12 What's it worth?
– let your head rule your heart

Condition

If the car you've been looking at is really bad, then you've probably not bothered to use the marking system in chapter 9 – 60 minute evaluation. You may not have even got as far as using that chapter at all!

If you did use the marking system in chapter 9 you'll know whether the car is in Excellent (maybe Concours), Good, Average or Poor condition or, perhaps, somewhere in-between these categories.

Many car magazines run a regular price guide, and there are specialist used car price guides available to the public. If you haven't bought the latest editions, do so now and compare their suggested values for the model you are thinking of buying: also look at the auction prices they're reporting. Some models will always be more sought-after than others. Trends can change too. The values published in the magazines and guides tend to vary from one magazine to another, as do their scales of condition, so read carefully the guidance notes they

There's plenty of price guide information available for these cars.

provide. Bear in mind that a car that is in truly magnificent condition or even a recent show winner, could be worth more than the highest scale published. Assuming that the car you have in mind is not in show/concours condition, then relate the level of condition that you judge the car to be in with the appropriate guide price. How does the figure compare with the asking price? Before you start haggling with the seller, consider what effect any variation from standard specification might have on the car's value. The list of extra cost options for these cars was expensive. and many were very expensive.

If you are buying from a dealer, remember there will be a dealer's premium on the price.

Desirable options/extras

As mentioned above these are additional options to standard equipment that might have been available when the car was new (at extra cost), or even later modifications, as many are still available for these cars. In many cases these can still command a higher price than cars without them.

Specific options that are beneficial and perhaps particularly expensive to retro-fit are cruise control, multi-media system (not necessarily with the TV as this is presently not worth having, but a DVD system is), xenon lighting, heated windscreen, sunroof, and much more.

The majority of exterior paint finishes were

Leather and walnut are still the most desirable trim options for those buying into the Jaguar brand.

metallic, so this should not affect price, but some colours are more popular than others, like blues, reds and silver. Walnut veneer is always the most popular, but many sporting models featured figured maple. Some later cars had an alloy finish, which was never that popular, and certainly not now in the aftermarket.

The vast majority of cars were equipped with alloy wheels. and many were or are now equipped with larger rims with low profile tyres. They look good, fill the wheelarches, and cost quite a lot to refurbish, so, if fitted, it is highly desirable to have them in excellent condition. Not all alloy wheels from other

Jaguar produced a whole range of accessory options for the X-Type, and for the modern estate car buyer these can come in very useful.

Jaguar models will fit these cars. A full-sized spare wheel is desirable for obvious reasons.

A trend has developed for owners to retro-fit styling enhancements. The most common changes include mesh grilles and under-grilles on the front of the car, different styles of alloy wheels, and chromed surrounds on some light units. Some owners have gone to the expense of fitting earlier cars with the bumper bars and radiator grille/surround from the later facelift.

Some companies are now offering electronic upgrades in the form of 'tweaked' ECUs, improved brakes, and much more. As long as they totally compatible with the existing technology, there shouldn't be a problem.

Many owners have complained about the poor headlamp lighting, and fitted higher wattage bulbs or aftermarket xenon type systems that provide a better quality of illumination.

Undesirable features

Most cars, even X-Types, are colour sensitive – or their owners are! White was never a popular colour, particularly in the cooler European climes, although it was very common in hot countries for obvious reasons. White is currently back in fashion, which may alter people's opinions. The earlier green colours are not that popular, and there have been so many greys around that they are considered common!

Some owners have personalised their cars with different colour schemes particular to the interior, revised trim, extra chrome, etc. Excellent for those who like such

The aftermarket fitting of accessories and trim is to an individual's choice, and can put off buyers.

things, but as these are generally very personal, they can prove a difficult selling point as they may not be to everyone's taste.

As far as the interiors are concerned, the lighter colours were – and still are – by far the most popular. Some of the later two-tone upholstery finishes didn't go down well, and are still an acquired taste. Walnut is more popular than grey-stained maple for the veneer, and the later alloy finish is certainly a rare find, and not so popular for this type of car.

LPG (liquid petroleum gas) is becoming a common modification for those concerned about using their cars regularly and rising petrol prices. Some of the best fitted systems only require the space in the spare wheel well, without infringing on boot accommodation, although this does mean fitting a space saver spare wheel in the boot, or doing without one entirely. Whilst LPG cuts down the cost of running these cars, it is a costly modification to make. Unless the car is destined to cover a relatively high mileage, it could take many years to recoup the value.

Very few people go to extremes with these cars, so fitting extensively modified engines etc is rare, usually doesn't improve the car's practicability for normal road use, and may eventually prove troublesome.

Striking a deal

Negotiate on the basis of your condition assessment, mileage, and fault rectification cost. Also take into account the car's specification. Be realistic about the value, but don't be completely intractable: a small compromise on the part of the vendor or buyer will often facilitate a deal at little real cost.

Some X-Types are taken to the extreme with lowered suspension, upgraded engines and transmissions, but is such a car to your personal taste?

It is not uncommon to find X-Types with modified interiors, again something to individual taste, and costly to put back to original specification.

13 Do you really want to restore?
– it'll take longer and cost more than you think

These X-Type models are not old enough or valuable enough to warrant restoration, and there is a plentiful supply of cars at prices to suit everyone's needs.

There are also numerous cars around that are available as Category D write-offs (cars that have been severely damaged beyond normal cost effective repair, but which have been rebuilt and made roadworthy). By the very nature of insurance claims and the high cost of labour, particularly to repair modern cars, makes many examples of this model hardly practical for an insurance company to sanction such a major repair. Such 'projects' can be purchased very cheaply and subsequently repaired, but will always retain their Category D status on the log sheet, and so are usually much cheaper than other examples. If you want a cheap car, these can be worth considering, but remember you will never get a reasonable price for such a car in re-sale.

To consider any major work on an X-Type can be daunting for the uninitiated, or even for a qualified mechanic, who may not have been trained on them or is not used to such sophisticated modern vehicles. If you have never refurbished a car before, or even done major work on a more conventional (older) model, you are best off avoiding an X-Type as a project. There will be a need for specialist tools, and in many cases expensive replacement parts. Even the franchised dealers, with their technically advanced diagnostic equipment, sometimes find the need to replace

No-one should consider restoring an X-Type – the cost will never be recouped – but such poor cars can become useful sources of replacement parts.

parts (at cost to the owner) unnecessarily. DIY servicing is possible, but other work needs serious consideration and a deep budget accordingly.

The one advantage is that Jaguar made a lot of these cars, and many have already gone to the dismantlers. With current legislation, dismantling is an art in itself, and the authorised companies that carry out such work hardly throw anything away. They clean, refurbish, and test many items, and make them available for purchase – much cheaper than going to your Jaguar dealership – and sometimes they come with a warranty.

These cars wear well inside, so it is unlikely that major work is required there although the soft leather on the driver's seat can suffer from constant scuffing. Today's modern upholstery repair specialists can work wonders, and many kits are available to do the work yourself, with new aftermarket sets of wood veneer readily available.

As many of these cars are already being scrapped because of their residual value versus repair costs, there is an increasing stream of good used components and trim to buy.

14 Paint problems
– bad complexion, including dimples, pimples and bubbles

Paint faults generally occur due to lack of protection/maintenance, or to poor preparation prior to a respray or touch-up. Some of the following conditions may be present in the car you're looking at:

Orange peel
This appears as an uneven paint surface, similar to the appearance of the skin of an orange. The fault is caused by the failure of atomized paint droplets to flow into each other when they hit the surface. It's sometimes possible to rub out the effect with proprietory paint cutting/ rubbing compound or very fine grades of abrasive paper. A respray may be necessary in severe cases. Consult a bodywork repairer/paint shop for advice on the particular car.

The standard of paint finish was very good from Jaguar, but look for general or localised matters like 'orange peeling', which takes away from the brilliant shine the car should have.

Cracking
Severe cases are likely to have been caused by too heavy an application of paint (or filler beneath the paint). Also, insufficient stirring of the paint before application can lead to the components being improperly mixed, and cracking can result. Incompatibility with the paint already on the panel can have a similar effect. To rectify the problem it is necessary to rub down to a smooth, sound finish before respraying the problem area.

Crazing
Sometimes the paint takes on a crazed rather than a cracked appearance when the problems mentioned under 'Cracking' are present. This problem can also be caused by a reaction between the underlying surface and the paint. Paint removal and respraying the problem area is usually the only solution.

This example shows paint shading where localised work has been done, not to the same standard as the rest of the car.

Blistering
Almost always caused by corrosion of the metal beneath the paint. Usually

perforation will be found in the metal and the damage will usually be worse than that suggested by the area of blistering. The metal will have to be repaired before repainting.

Micro blistering
Usually the result of an economy respray where inadequate heating has allowed moisture to settle on the car before spraying. Consult a paint specialist, but usually damaged paint will have to be removed before partial or full respraying. Can also be caused by car covers that don't 'breathe'.

Fading
Some colours, especially reds, are prone to fading if subjected to strong sunlight for long periods without the benefit of polish protection. Sometimes proprietary paint restorers and/or paint cutting/rubbing compounds will retrieve the situation. Often a respray is the only real solution.

Peeling
Often a problem with metallic paintwork when the sealing laquer becomes damaged and begins to peel off. Poorly applied paint may also peel. The remedy is to strip and start again!

Dimples
Dimples in the paintwork are caused by the residue of polish (particularly silicone types) not being removed properly before respraying. Paint removal and repainting is the only solution.

Dents
Small dents are usually easily cured by the 'Dentmaster', or equivalent process, that sucks or pushes out the dent (as long as the paint surface is still intact). Companies offering dent removal services usually come to your home: consult your telephone directory.

15 Problems due to lack of use
– just like their owners, X-Types need exercise!

Cars, like humans, are at their most efficient if they exercise regularly. A run of at least twenty miles is needed just to thoroughly warm up a modern car like the X-Type and good, regular use is strongly recommended.

Seized components
Pistons in brake calipers, slave and master cylinders can seize. Handbrakes (parking brakes) can seize if the cables and linkages rust, or are not lubricated and the handbrake should be left off during long storage.

Fluids
Uninhibited coolant can corrode internal waterways. Lack of the correct mix of antifreeze in the coolant can severely damage an engine. Silt settling and solidifying can cause overheating. Brake fluid absorbs water from the atmosphere and should be renewed every two years. Old fluid with a high water content can cause corrosion and pistons/calipers to seize (freeze) and can cause brake failure when the water turns to vapour near hot braking components,

Tyre problems
Tyres that have had the weight of the car on them in a single position for some time will develop flat spots, resulting in some (usually temporary) vibration. The tyre walls may have cracks or (blister-type) bulges, meaning new tyres are needed. Tyres do not have a infinite life even if the tread wear is low. Modern alloy wheels can go oval with long-term storage of a car in one position.

Suspension
With lack of use, the suspension can lose its elasticity or even seize. Creaking, groaning, and stiff suspension are signs of this problem.

Rubber and plastic
Radiator hoses may have perished and split, possibly resulting in the loss of all coolant. Window and door seals can harden and leak. Gaitors/boots can crack. Wiper blades will harden.

Electrics
The battery will be of little use if it has not been charged for many months. These cars will always have a 'drain' from their electronics systems, which will slowly flatten the battery if a 'battery saver' device is not fitted. Earthing/grounding problems are common when the connections have corroded. Wiring insulation can harden and fail.
    The modern electronic systems in the X-Type do not like lack of use.
Beware long term storage in a country garage where rodents can gain access. They have a habit of chewing at electrical cables or even storing their winter food in such diverse areas as air cleaners and air-conditioning systems.

A car that has been parked up for months in a garage where rodents decided to store their hibernation food in the heater unit. A costly repair followed!

Batteries are one of the first things to suffer with long-term storage, so it is best to either disconnect completely and remove from the car, or attach a trickle charger to maintain condition.

Rotting exhaust system

Exhaust gas contains a high water content, so exhaust systems corrode very quickly from the inside when the car is not used. This even applies to stainless steel systems internally and, in some cases, externally.

16 The Community
– key people, organisations and companies in the X-Type world

The franchised Jaguar dealer network still maintains many of these cars, and is happy to continue looking after older examples. Jaguar Cars still supplies the majority of parts required. There is now a strong network of independent Jaguar specialists who also maintain these vehicles at reasonable cost, and spares businesses, already well known for the supply of parts for classic Jaguars, are now also catering for the X-Types. There are also a few authorized dismantlers who can supply refurbished second-hand parts.

The cars are also very well supported by Jaguar marque clubs and internet sites, so there is ample opportunity to find out more from existing owners and seek advice when required. And finally, even though these cars are still relatively new, some insurance companies are already treating them as cherished vehicles, thus allowing owners to obtain reasonable car insurance.

Clubs

The Jaguar Drivers' Club
18 Stuart Street
Luton, Bedfordshire LU1 2SL
Tel: +44 (0)1582 419332
www.jaguardriver.co.uk
The oldest Jaguar marque club based in the UK, catering for all models, with a monthly magazine, insurance scheme and a good overseas network.

The Jaguar Enthusiasts' Club offers annual seminars where owners can learn more about the cars.

The Jaguar Enthusiasts' Club
Abbeywood Office Park
Emma Chris Way
Filton, Bristol BS34 7JU
Tel: +4 (0)1179 698186
www.jec.org.uk
The world's largest Jaguar club catering for all models with a special very active forum and technical seminars for X-Type owners. 132-page full colour monthly magazine, insurance schemes, technical advice, specialist tools supply and hire, plus events, tours and runs.

There is a lot of interest now in X-Types on internet forum sites, the Jaguar clubs taking more of an interest and congregating at events.

Jaguar Clubs of North America
C/o Nelson Rath
1000 Glenbrook
Anchorage. KY 40223
Tel: +1 502 244 1672
www.jcna.com
Umbrella organisation for US-based Jaguar clubs, with an events calendar and monthly magazine.

Jaguar Heritage
C/o Jaguar Heritage Archive
The Heritage Motor Centre
Banbury Road,
Gaydon, Warwickshire CV35 OBJ
Tel: +44 (0)1926 645082/3
www.jaguarheritage.org
Holder of the official Jaguar Cars archive, with information available on car
build details, Heritage Certificate supply, CDs available on service/maintenance
information, plus photographic library.

Specialist independent X-Type service/maintenance providers

XJK Independent Jaguar Specialists Ltd
Albany Road
Newcastle under Lyme,
Staffordshire ST5 9EJ
Tel: +44 (0)1782 613434
www.xjkltd.co.uk

Independent specialists are now looking after X-Types, providing a valuable service at cost-effective prices.

David Marks Garages
Unit 36, Wilford & North
Nottingham Industrial Estate
Ruddington Lane,
Nottingham NG11 7EP
Tel: +44 (0)115 982 2808
www.davidmarksgarages.co.uk

R.G Bate (Engineering) Ltd
501 Cleveland Street,
Birkenhead, Cheshire CH41 3EF
Tel: +44 (0)151 653 6765

Simon March & Co
Scoreby Lodge, Hull road.
Dunnington, York YO19 5LR
Tel: +44 (0)1904 489821

Philip Welch Specialist Cars
Hull Road,
Dunnington, York YO19 5LP
Tel: +44 (0)1904 488252
www.philipwelch.co.uk

Nene Jag Specialists
8 Harvester Way, Fengate
Peterborough PE 1 5UT
Tel: +44 (0)1733 349042
www.nenejags.co.uk

Les Pauls Jaguar Specialists
Unit 7, Anderson Road Industrial Estate,
Woodford Green, Essex IG8 8ET
Tel: +44 (0)208 551 8537
www.lespauls.motors.co.uk

Parts Suppliers
S.N.G Barratt Ltd
Stourbridge Road
Bridgnorth, Shropshire WV15 6AP
Tel: +44 (0)1746 765432
www.sngbarratt.com

XJK Independent Jaguar Specialists Ltd
Albany Road
Newcastle under Lyme, Staffordshire ST5 9EJ
Tel: +44 (0)1782 613434
www.xjkltd.co.uk

Eurojag (refurbished parts)
Sovereign House, Neasham Road, Hurworth Moor
Darlington, Co. Durham DL2 1QH
Tel: +44 (0)1325 722777
www.eurojag.com

Modifications & Upgrades
Adamesh
Unit 11, Acacia Close, Cherrycourt Way
Leighton Buzzard, Bedfordshire LU7 4QE
Tel: +44 (0)1525 852419
www.adamesh.co.uk

Racing Green Cars
Station Road West,
Ashvale, Hampshire GU12 5QD
Tel: +44 (0)1252 544888
www.racinggreencars.com

Useful sources of information
Jaguar World Monthly magazine
The independent monthly magazine from Kelsey Publishing, with regular features on
these models.

Jaguar – All the Cars
By the author of this title, the all-in-one guide to the history and development of all
the Jaguar models, with a special chapter on the X-Type models.

17 Vital statistics
– essential data at your fingertips

Production figures

2.0-litre petrol saloons	49,762
2.0-litre petrol estates	1,587
2.0-litre diesel saloons	55,615
2.0-litre diesel estates	16,747
2.2-litre diesel sal/est*	31,373
2.5-litre petrol saloons	99,939
2.5-litre petrol estates	4,306
3.0-litre petrol saloons	91,595
3.0-litre petrol estates	4,382
Total	355,306

* The Jaguar Halewood factory where the X-Types were produced did not differentiate in its final figures between the independent totals for 2.2-litre diesel cars and estates.

Technical specifications

2.0-litre petrol engine
2,099cc 81.6mm x 66.8mm six-cylinder
157bhp @ 6800rpm & 148 lb/ft @ 4100rpm

2.0-litre diesel engine
1,998cc 86mm x 86mm 4-cylinder
128bhp @ 3800rpm & 243lb/ft @ 1800rpm

2.2-litre diesel engine
2,198cc 86mm x 94.6mm 4-cylinder
155bhp @ 3500rpm & 360lb/ft @ 1800rpm

2.5-litre petrol engine
2,495cc six-cylinder 24 valve engine
81.6mm x 79.5mm 194bhp @ 6800rpm & 180lb/ft @ 3000rpm

3.0-litre petrol engine
2,967cc 6 cyinder 24 valve engine
89mm x 79.5mm 231bhp @ 6800rpm & 209 lb/ft @ 3000rpm

Transmissions

5-speed all synchromesh manual transmission
6-speed all synchromesh manual transmission
Ford 5-speed automatic transmission

Dimensions

Length	183in (4648.6mm) saloons/186in (4724mm) estates
Width	68in (1727mm) all cars
Height	53in (1346mm) saloons/58in (1473mm) estates
Weight	2.0p 3197lb (1450kg) saloons/3328lb (1510kg) estates
	2.0d 3311lb (1501kg) saloons/3473lb (1575kg) estates
	2.2d 3473lb (1575kg) saloons/3635lb (1648kg) estates
	2.5 3428lb (1555kg) saloons/3538lb (1605kg) estates
	3.0 3428lb (1555kg) saloons/3538lb (1605kg) estates

Suspension

Front: independent double wishbones, coil springs.
Rear: independent double wishbones, coil springs.

Brakes

All round discs, ventilated, power assisted with ABS.

Steering

Variable power assisted rack and pinion with adjustable steering column

Wheels

A wide choice of alloy wheels dependent on model and individual order:
16in (406mm)
17in (432mm)
18in (457mm

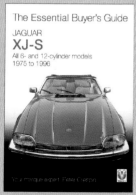

The Essential Buyer's Guide
JAGUAR
XJ-S
All 6- and 12-cylinder models
1975 to 1996

Your marque expert: Peter Crespin

978-1-84584-161-4
£9.99/$19.95

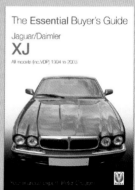

The **Essential** Buyer's Guide
Jaguar/Daimler
XJ40
All models 1986 to 1994

Your marque expert: Peter Crespin

978-1-84584-192-8
£9.99/$19.95

The **Essential** Buyer's Guide
Jaguar/Daimler
XJ
All models (inc.VDP) 1994 to 2003

Your marque expert: Peter Crespin

978-1-84584-200-0
£9.99/$19.95

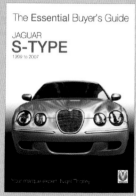

The **Essential** Buyer's Guide
JAGUAR
S-TYPE
1999 to 2007

Your marque expert: Nigel Thorley

978-1-845844-45-5
£9.99/$19.95

The **Essential** Buyer's Guide
JAGUAR
XK8 & XKR
1996-2005

Your marque expert: Nigel Thorley

978-1-845843-59-5
£9.99/$19.95

The **Essential** Buyer's Guide
Jaguar
XJ6, XJ8 & XJR
All 2003 to 2009 (X-350) models including Daimler

Your marque expert: Nigel Thorley

978-1-845844-34-9
£9.99/$19.95

The Essential Buyer's Guide™ series ...

978-1-845840-22-8   978-1-845840-26-6   978-1-845840-29-7   978-1-845840-77-8   978-1-845840-99-0   978-1-845841-01-0   978-1-845841-07-2   978-1-845841-13-3

978-1-845841-19-5   978-1-845841-34-8   978-1-845841-35-5   978-1-845841-36-2   978-1-845841-38-6   978-1-845841-46-1   978-1-845841-47-8   978-1-845841-61-4

978-1-845841-63-8   978-1-845841-65-2   978-1-845841-88-1   978-1-845841-92-8   978-1-845842-00-0   978-1-845842-04-8   978-1-845842-05-5   978-1-845842-31-4

978-1-845842-70-3   978-1-845842-81-9   978-1-845842-83-3   978-1-845842-84-0   978-1-845842-87-1   978-1-845842-90-1   978-1-845843-03-8   978-1-845843-07-6

978-1-845843-09-0   978-1-845843-16-8   978-1-845843-29-8   978-1-845843-30-4   978-1-845843-34-2   978-1-845843-38-0   978-1-845843-39-7

£9.99 / $19.95 (prices subject to change, p&p extra).
For more details visit www.veloce.co.uk or email info@veloce.co.uk

... don't buy a vehicle until you've read one of these!

Index